FISHING

BY

Roy Marsden

ILLUSTRATED BY

Shelley Page

MACDONALD

First published 1979
Reprinted 1980

Macdonald Educational Ltd
Holywell House
Worship Street
London EC2A 2EN

©Macdonald Educational 1979
ISBN 0 356 06323 2 (paperback)
ISBN 0 356 06363 1 (hardback)

Printed by New Interlitho,
Milan, Italy

About this book

This book has been carefully planned to help you become an expert. Look for the special pages to find the information you need. **RECOGNITION** pages, with a **bright yellow flash** in the top right-hand corner, contain all the essential information to know and remember. **PROJECT** pages, with a **grey border,** suggest some interesting ideas for things to do and make. At the end of the book there is a useful **REFERENCE SECTION.**

Freshwater fishing

This boy is going on a day's fishing. His tackle and equipment are stored inside the wicker basket.

Freshwater fishing is fun. It offers something for everyone, and combines peace and quiet with action and excitement. 'Freshwater' simply means any inland water which is not affected by the salt tides of the sea.

Types of fish

There are two main kinds of freshwater fish: game fish and coarse fish. Game fish are members of the salmon family: salmon, trout and grayling. All other fish are called coarse fish, from the old phrase 'in course' meaning ordinary or usual.

Licences and permits

Wherever you are fishing you will need a rod licence from the Area Water Authority, and sometimes another permit, a club membership or day ticket. Buy them from your local tackle shop or fishing club.

No angling is allowed during the fish breeding seasons, or '**close seasons**'. For coarse fish and grayling, the close season is 15 March-15 June; for salmon, 1 November-31 January; for brown trout, 1 October-end of February. The close season for rainbow trout varies from areas to area. There is no close season for coarse fish in Scotland or Ireland.

Cruelty

Nobody can claim that fish enjoy being caught. But if they are handled properly, the fish feel discomfort rather than pain. Always return coarse fish to the water unharmed.

Using a landing net makes bringing in a fish much easier. It is also kinder to the fish. Remember: a fish that is properly hooked, played and landed will not feel pain.

Rods and tackle

The rod
A three-piece rod of hollow fibre-glass will suit most kinds of freshwater fishing. Choose a length to suit your height and strength: probably 3-5 metres is best.

Put the rod together from the top joint downwards. Look along the rings to check they are in line. Take the rod apart from the bottom joint upwards.

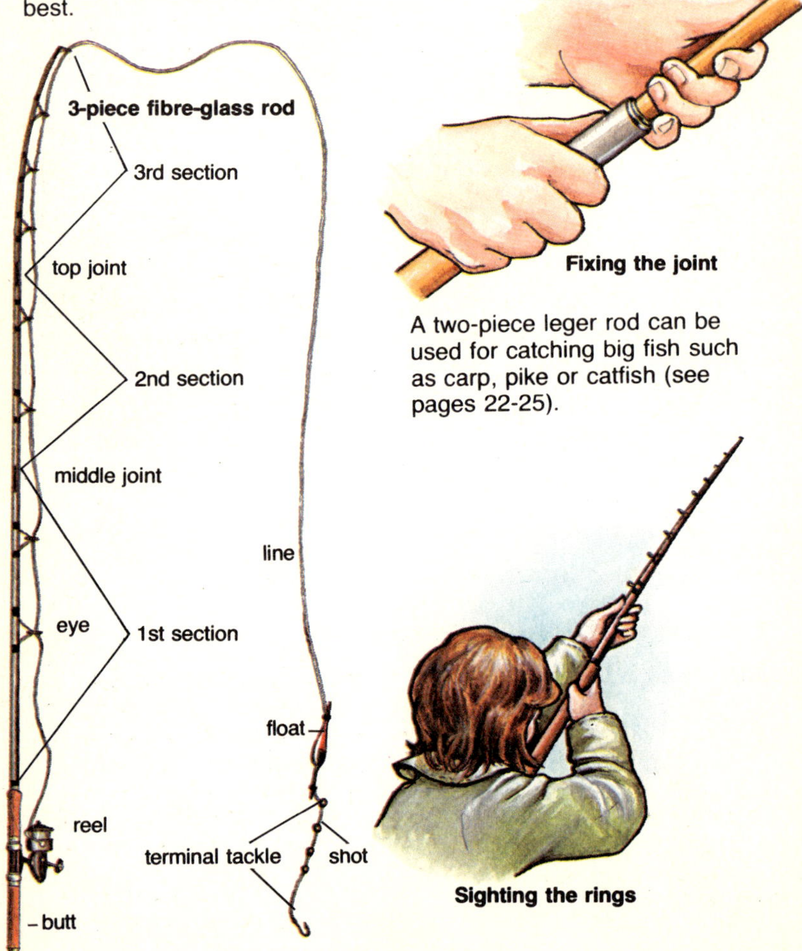

Fixing the joint

A two-piece leger rod can be used for catching big fish such as carp, pike or catfish (see pages 22-25).

Sighting the rings

The reel

The fixed spool reel is the most popular type. When the handle is turned, the 'bale' arm revolves and winds the line onto the spool. The spool moves up and down to spread the line evenly. Spare spools can carry different strengths of line.

The centre pin reel simply winds the line onto a revolving drum. It is more old-fashioned but has certain advantages (see page 32).

Fixed spool reel

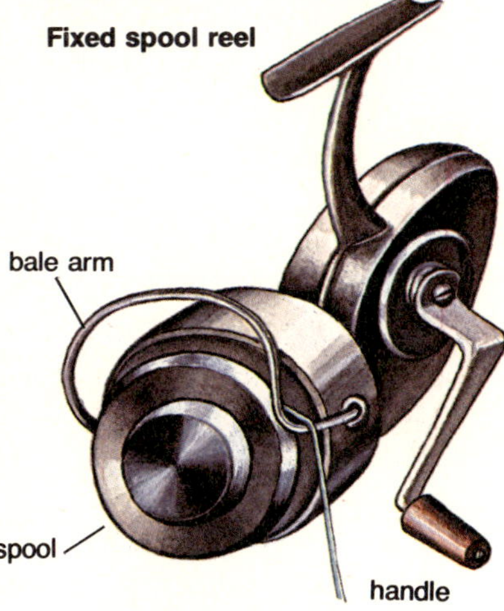

Centre pin reel

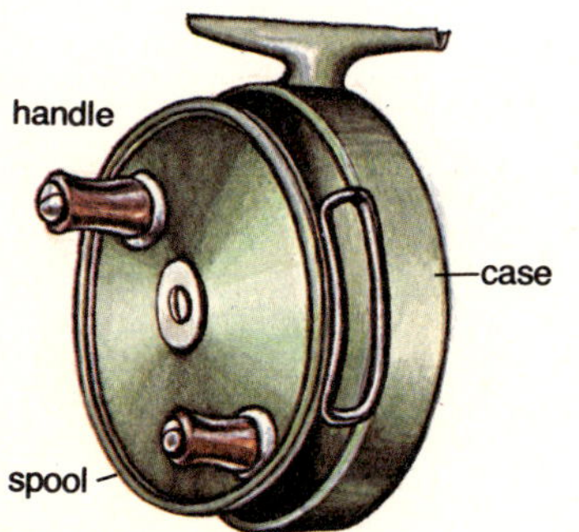

The line

Most line is made of man-made fibre such as nylon. It is strong, but tricky to knot. It is also weakened by being knotted and having shot fixed on to it, so cut off the last metre or so after each fishing trip.

Hooks

Hooks come in two basic shapes: 'round bend' and 'crystal'. They can be bought with a cast (a length of nylon line) already attached. Hooks without a cast are fixed to the line either by an 'eye' or a flat 'spade'.

There are treble hooks, and worm tackle made up of several hooks. Snap tackle is used for deadbait.

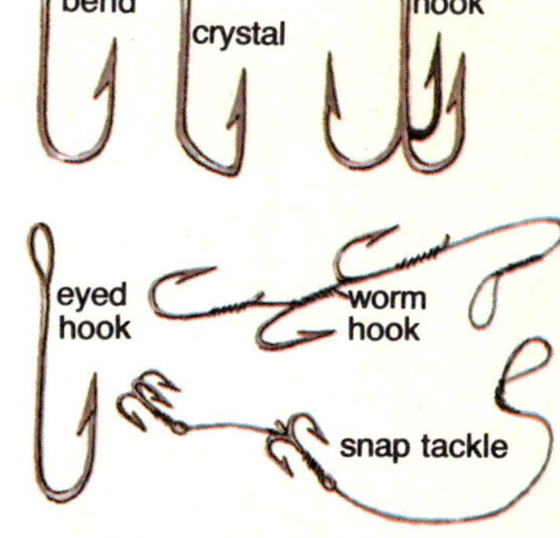

Hook sizes   Single hooks come in sizes numbering from one upwards. Number one is the biggest, two is slightly smaller and so on. The size you need depends on the size of your bait and of the fish you hope to catch.

A selection of hooks in sizes 8-14 will serve most purposes.

Clothing and equipment

The right kind of clothing for fishing is very important. A full day in the open air can bring all kinds of weather, so be prepared for changes. You may need protection from wind, rain and sunshine; so you should be ready for all three.

A **woolly hat** will help to keep your head warm on a cold day.

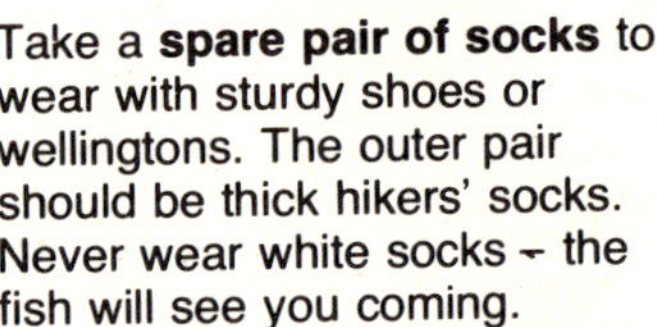

Take a **spare pair of socks** to wear with sturdy shoes or wellingtons. The outer pair should be thick hikers' socks. Never wear white socks – the fish will see you coming.

A **'cagoule'** (lightweight plastic overjacket that folds up into a small pack), anorak or fishing jacket is essential. It will protect you from wind and rain.

Carry a **spare pullover** in case you get cold. Remember that layers of clothing help to retain body heat. They are also easy to shed if the day suddenly turns warm.

Fingerless gloves are useful in cold weather. They will keep your hands warm but leave your fingers free for delicate jobs like tying knots and baiting up.

Equipment
The landing net and keep net should be as big as you can afford, with small, knotless mesh so as not to damage the fish.

Use a wicker or steel-framed canvas tackle basket. Hooks, floats, weights etc. can be kept in a plastic tackle box with foldaway compartments.

Rod rests should be sturdy so that they don't bend when pushed into the bank. Disgorgers are for removing hooks. Bait can be carried in plastic containers with airholes.

wicker tackle basket

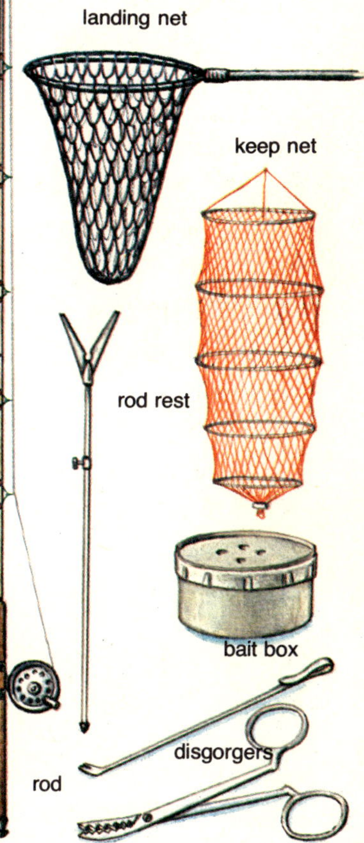

Bait

Groundbait

Groundbait is used to attract fish to a fishing spot. You can make a basic groundbait by scooping out the inside of a loaf of bread. Soak it in water and mash it to a pulp. (Save the crust for hookbait.) Squeeze out the surplus water and add bran, dried breadcrumbs or chicken meal. The finished groundbait should be just damp enough to hold together when squeezed into balls.

At the waterside, you add bits of your hookbait to each ball: maggots, worms or cheese. You may need to weight the ball with a stone, or soil from the bank, to get it to the bottom in a current. Throw it well upstream of the spot you intend to fish.

Throwing a ball of groundbait into the water is a good way to attract fish to your fishing spot.

A maggot correctly hooked. Notice how the hook goes through the frill, rather than the body of the maggot.

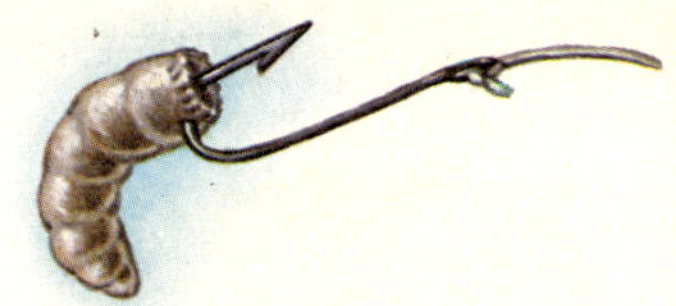

Hookbait from shop or larder

Maggots should be hooked through the frill at the blunt end. Use them singly or in bunches. When they turn into chrysalises they are called 'casters'.

Hemp-seed makes another good hookbait. Cook gently until the grains split. Put the hook into the white slit and nip the shell hard to hold it. But remember that on some waters, hemp-seed is banned.

All kinds of bait attract fish. Bread can be used as **paste** (kneaded with water into a stiff dough), as **flake** (pieces squeezed and hooked through the middle) or as **crust**. Cheese can be used in chunks, or mixed with butter to make a paste. Try sausage or luncheon meat, wheat, or even a partly boiled potato.

Hookbait

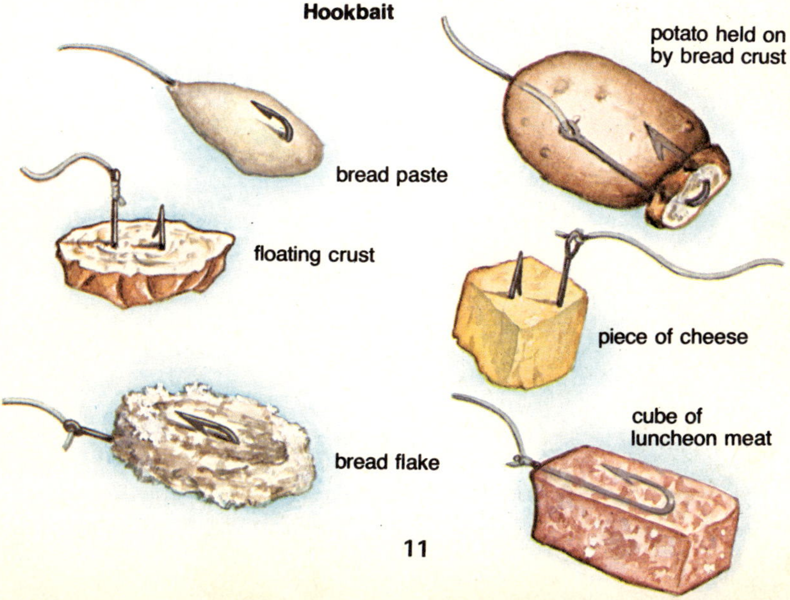

Bait from outdoors

You can collect different baits from the garden, from hedgerows, and even from the water itself.

Slugs, woodlice, caterpillars, grasshoppers and snails all make good bait, so does soft fruit.

Worms are excellent bait. Collect bloodworms from ditches or water butts and use them on very small hooks.

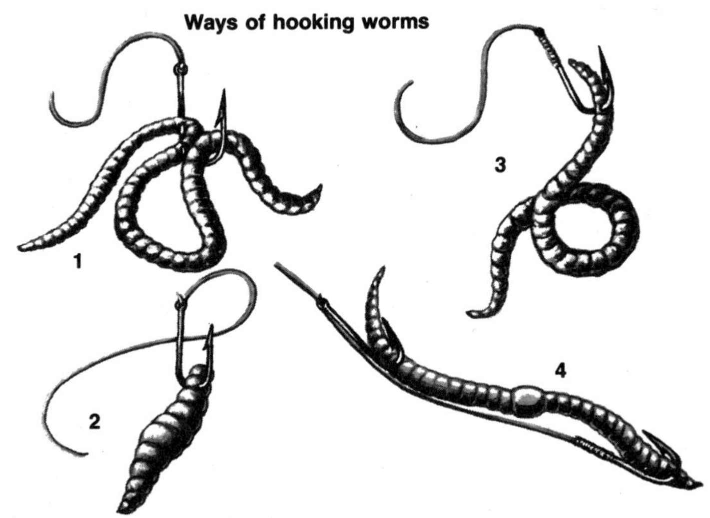

Hook red worms through the middle (1) or the tail (2).

Hook lobworms through the tail (3) or with two-hook tackle (4).

Earwigs and grubs

To collect earwigs, place a flowerpot filled with straw on a stake in a flowerbed. In autumn, shake a bunch of elderberries: it will be full of earwigs.

Dig up dock plants and look for the white dock grub. Collect wasp grubs, but don't try to do so without expert help: the adult wasps don't like it.

Bait from the water

From the water itself you can collect caddis grubs, or use the flesh of snails, mussels or crayfish. Always collect them in a landing net: the water may be deep.

Dead fish can be used as leger or spinning baits. Silkweed, which grows on underwater stonework, is also good bait. Collect it by drawing your hook through it.

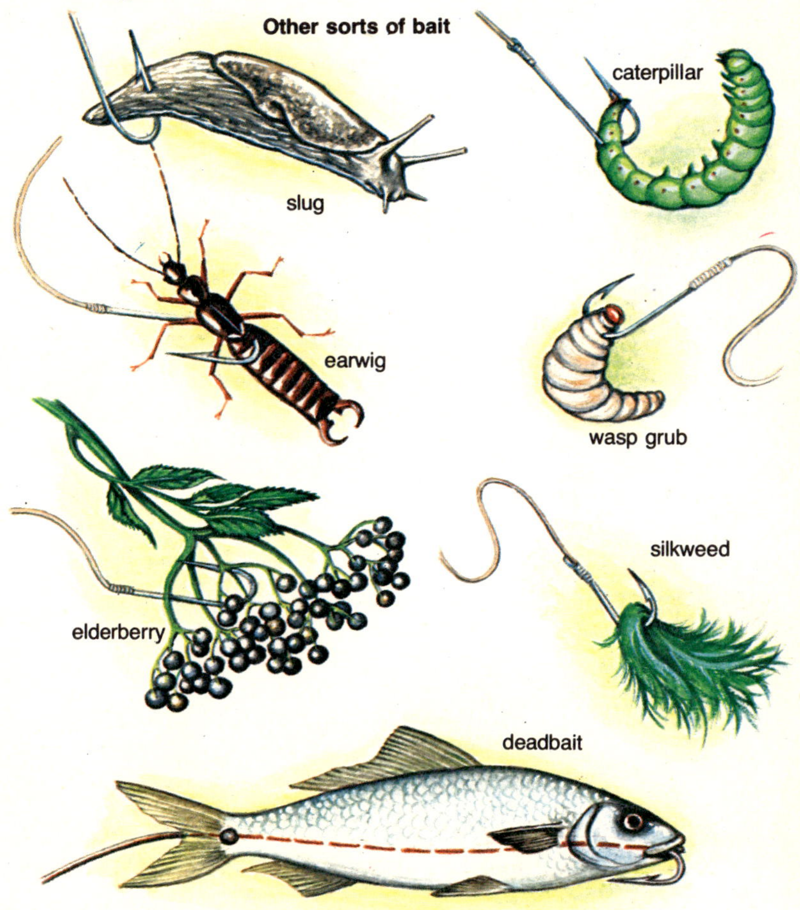

Breeding maggots

1. Put a piece of raw liver in a pan of damp sand or bran. Leave in a cool place such as a shed, garage or shrubbery.

3. Within 10 days the maggots will be fully grown. Transfer them to a tin of damp sand to clean them.

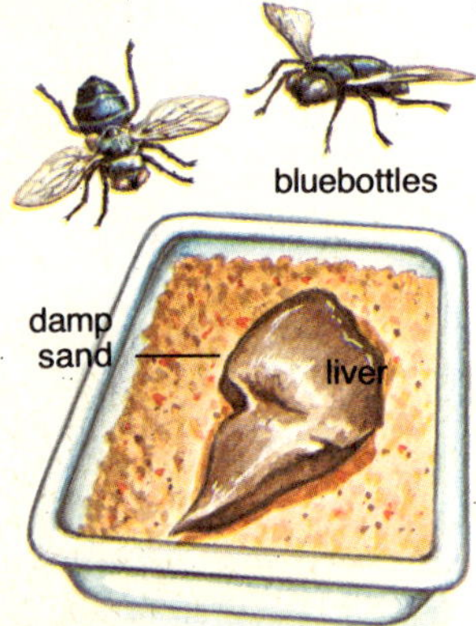

4. After a few days, separate the maggots from the sand with a fine sieve (obtainable from tackle shops).

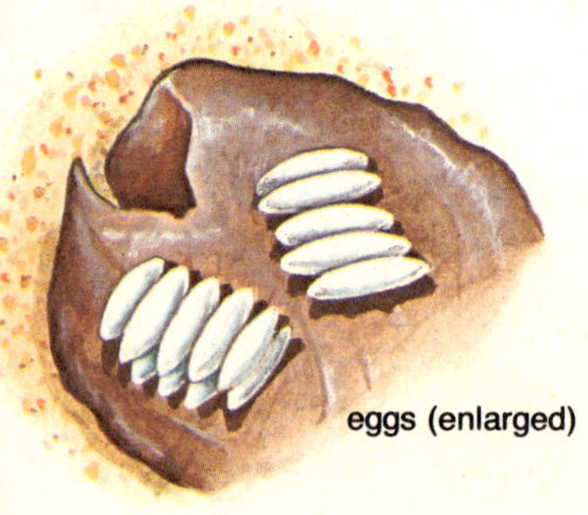
eggs (enlarged)

2. The bluebottles will lay clusters of tiny white eggs on the meat. Cover the pan and leave it somewhere cool. The maggots will hatch in 3-4 days.

5. Put the maggots into a plastic bag (as above), making sure that it is securely tied. Keep it in the salad drawer of a refrigerator. This stops the maggots hatching out in warm weather. But first make sure your mother knows about them!

Making a wormery

1. Choose a small patch in the garden. Remove all stones and dig in some soaked and shredded newspaper. Make a square frame from old bits of wood. Push the frame into the ground.

3. Keep the wormery moist. Soon the worms will start breeding. From then on, just peel back the sack to collect your bait. If you have no garden, make the wormery out of a wooden box.

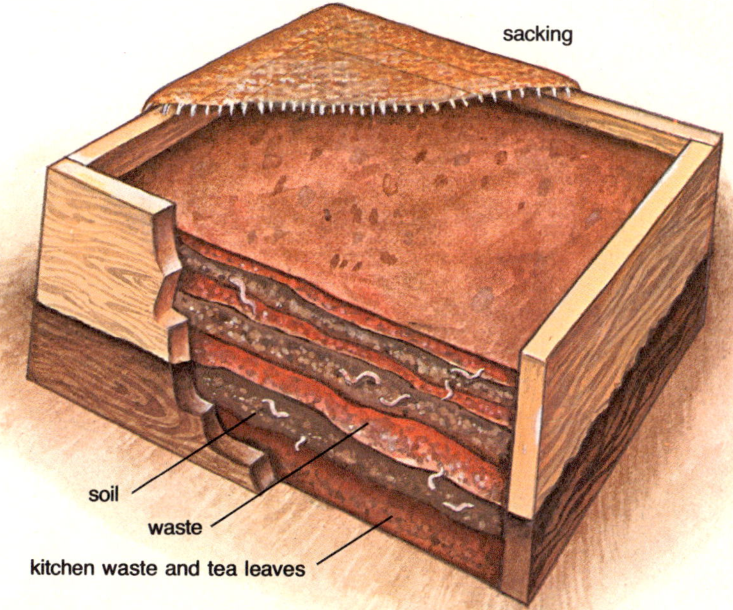

2. Empty all your old tea leaves into the frame. Dig in garden and kitchen waste, such as grass cuttings and peelings, and keep adding shredded newspapers. Every few centimetres add a thin layer of soil. Stock the frame with worms. Cover with a sack.

4. The worms will be a bit soft. Try to collect them a week before they are needed. Put them in a tin of florist's moss with airholes at **both** ends. Turn the tin upside down twice a day. The worms will keep burrowing through the moss, toughening their skins in the process.

Where to find fish

Looking at the water

Most fish like gentle waters away from strong currents. (The barbel is an exception: it likes fast water.) Food is carried along by strong currents, but it tends to collect in quieter spots. Besides, fish are shy. They like to have good cover.

You can expect to find fish around weedbeds, and lily pads, as well as under overhanging trees and near bridges, piers, rocks and islands. The picture below shows some likely spots for good fishing.

A. Runs between and beside weedbeds.
B. The mouth of a smaller 'feeder' stream.
C. Around the piling of a jetty or landing stage.
D. Shallow runs near the bank (mainly for smaller fish).
E. Behind rocks and boulders.
F. In eddies.
G. Around and under lily pads.
H. Around a fallen tree or similar obstruction.
I. Under overhanging bushes (particularly for chub).
J. Behind islands.
K. Around and behind rushes (particularly for pike).
L. On the inside of a bend in the river.

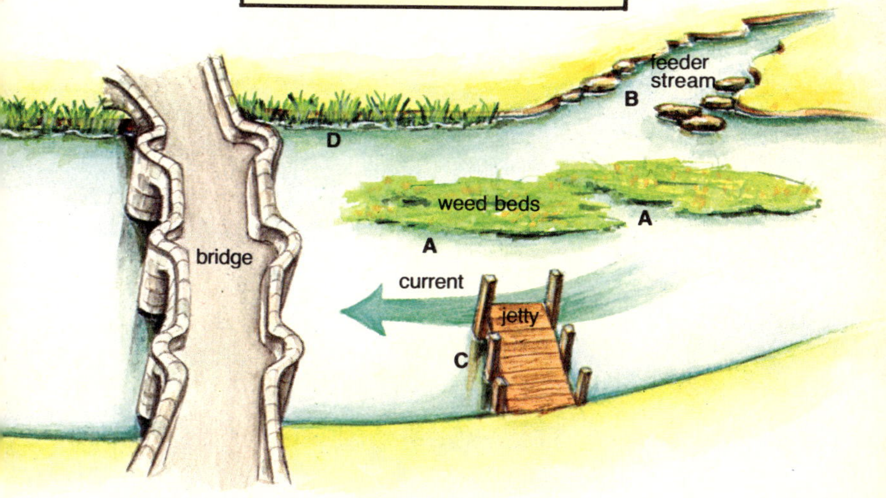

Types of fish

The surface of the water on a warm day is full of life.

Anglers divide freshwater fish into three main types according to the depth of water the fish like best: surface feeders, wanderers, and bottom feeders.

Surface feeders
The surface feeders seek their food in the top half-metre of water – an area full of activity, especially in the warmer months. Water plants grow towards the light, bringing with them the tiny creatures which live among their leaves. Larvae hatch on the surface, and food, such as insects and seeds, is constantly falling from above. The surface area makes a good hunting ground for bleak, dace, rudd and chub.

Wandering fish

All fish wander in search of food, but some roam
more than others. To catch these wanderers the
angler must seek them out. He may find them at any
water level.

Pike, perch and zander are wanderers. They feed
mainly on other fish and have to go looking for their
prey. The game fish (salmon, trout and grayling) are
also wanderers. They will bite at small creatures
such as flies, grubs, shrimps and worms.

Bottom feeders

The bottom of a river or lake is a rich feeding
ground. A large number of fish spend most of their
time there. Some give themselves away to the angler
by disturbing the bottom.

Carp feed in clouds of mud and bubbles. A shoal
of bream sends up thousands of bubbles and
discolours the water. Tench give off streams of tiny
bubbles which rise to the surface in a straight line.

A shoal of bream feeding on
the bottom.

The surface feeders

Bleak, dace, rudd and chub are the main surface feeders. For the first three, fish lightly with small hooks and bait. The chub will take heavier tackle, but he is very cautious: you must tempt him by floating the bait gently.

The illustrations on the opposite page show some of the most common clues to look out for when identifying your catch.

The parts of a fish
You will find it easier to identify your catch if you learn the names of the main features, as shown below. Most of them appear in some form on all fish, whether surface feeders, bottom feeders or wanderers.

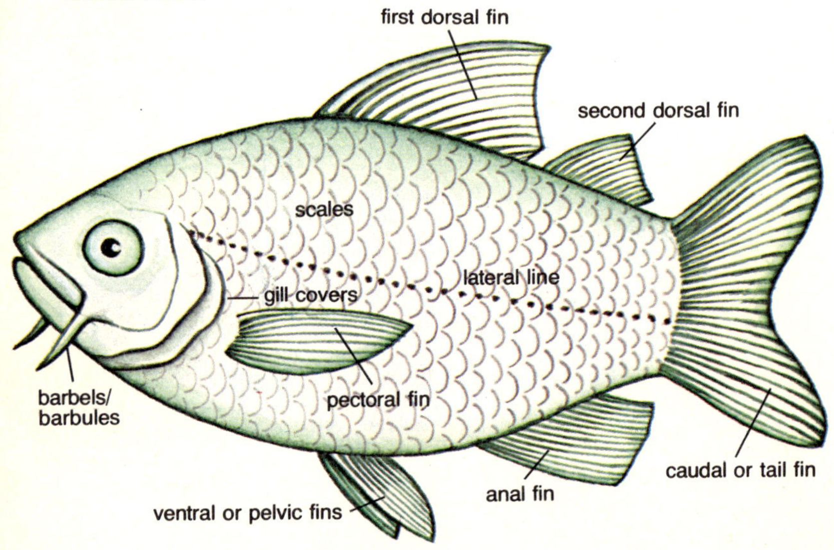

Dace/chub

Dace are sometimes confused
with small chub.

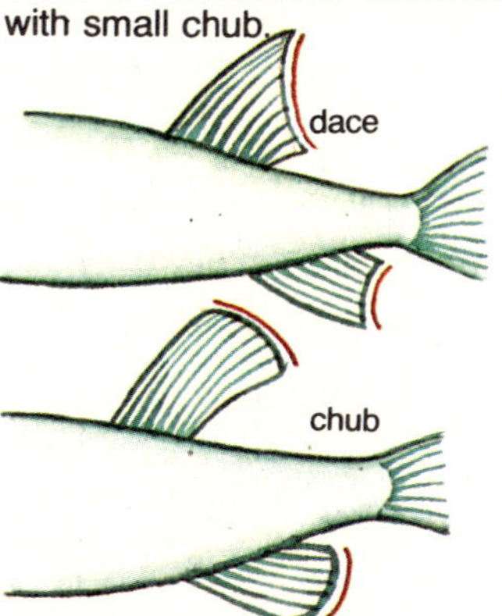

But the dace has concave
edges to its dorsal and anal fins,
while the chub's are convex.

Rudd/roach

The rudd is sometimes confused
with the roach. But it is bulkier.

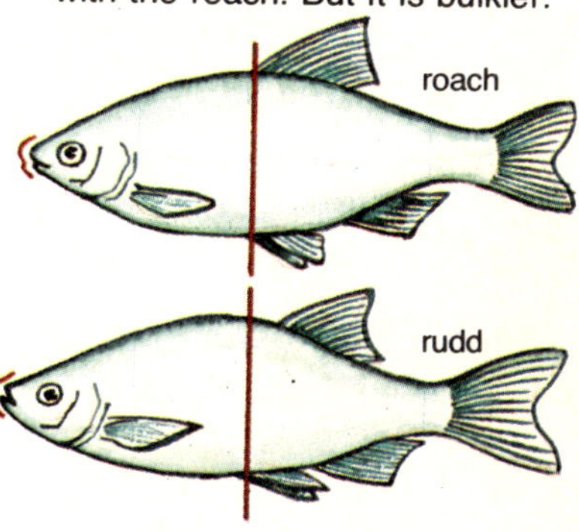

Compare also the lower jaw of
rudd and roach. Compare also
the position of their dorsal fins.

Bleak

A small silver fish with a
greenish back. It feeds in shoals
at the surface of moving water.
Will take almost any small bait:
maggots, casters, bread,
cheese, hemp-seed, and
artificial flies.

Dace

Lively silver fish. Likes clear,
running water. Takes maggots,
small worms, hemp-seed, bread
paste and small natural baits.
Try also small artificial flies and
tiny flashy spinners.

Chub

A cautious fish with pale bronze
sides. It likes moving water
especially under trees. Takes
almost anything: worms,
maggots, bread, cheese,
sausage, meat, soft fruit and
vegetables.

Rudd

Bulkier than average fish with
olive green back, gold-bronze
flanks, scarlet fins and bright red
eyes. Likes still or slow water.
Takes maggots, casters, bread,
worms, cheese, hemp-seed, and
wheat.

Wandering fish

Perch
A handsome and greedy fish, with an unmistakable, spiky dorsal fin. Its back is green, its flanks green-gold and striped with black. Roams in packs in search of larvae, insects, worms, snails and small fish.

Takes maggots, worms, wobbled deadbaits, small plugs, spinners and spoons.

Pike
Long, lean and evil-looking. Back is dark green, flanks lighter with yellow bars. Eats fish, frogs, voles and young water birds. A solitary fish.

Lurks near cover in still or slow water and makes a short dash for its prey. Also roams in search of food. Will take deadbaits, plugs, spinners, spoons and moving worms.

Zander
Shaped like a pike, but with a perch-like dorsal fin. Often mistakenly called the pike-perch. Smaller zanders feed in shoals, but larger ones hunt alone.

Imported into Britain and is still only common in the Great Ouse river system. Will take deadbaits and strips of fish legered or wobbled. Also attracted to small, flashy plugs.

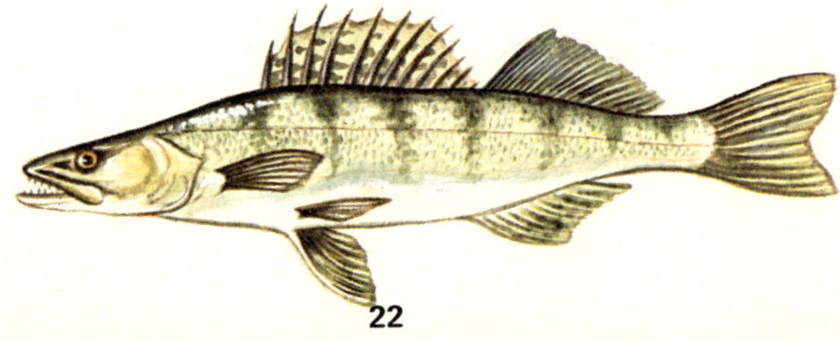

Three of the wanderers are coarse fish: pike, perch and zander. Three are game fish: salmon, trout and grayling. Fishing for the wanderers is an active pursuit, and often involves either spinning or fly fishing. The angler has to *hunt* the fish.

Grayling

Silvery, with shimmering overtones of purple, green and yellow. A member of the salmon family but spawns at the same time as coarse fish.

Will take wet and dry flies, maggots, wasp grubs, small red worms and grasshoppers.

Trout

The brown trout varies enormously in colour, size, shape and spotting patterns. The rainbow trout was imported into Britain and has a speckled tail and a narrow red band on each flank.

Brown and rainbow trout like both still and running water. They will take dry fly, wet fly, spinners, spun deadbaits, crayfish, shrimps and worms – often the most effective bait.

Salmon

A big silver fish, spends most of its life at sea and only returns to fresh water to spawn. Swims upriver, stopping to rest in quiet pools and bays.

The salmon does not feed in the river, but will snap at anglers' offerings. Takes spinners, wet flies, worms and shrimps.

The bottom feeders

Most bottom feeders move in shoals, feeding like cattle grazing on the bed of a lake or river. When fishing for bottom feeders, it is important to find the exact depth of the water. Your hookbait should lie on the bed itself.

Barbel
A powerful fighter, likes fast, shallow water. Green or bronze in colour. Dorsal fin has a saw-toothed spine. Takes almost anything: worms, bread, cheese, sausage, silkweed, deadbait.

Bream
Likes slow, spacious waters. Colour is bronze. Deep, flat and very slimy body. Very shy. Takes worms, cheese, bread, maggots, sausage, freshwater mussels. Needs plenty of groundbait.

Silver bream
A much smaller relative of the common or bronze bream. Has the same shape, but colour is greeny silver and the eyes are large and round. Takes the same baits as the bronze bream.

Carp
Strong, gentle fish of slow or still waters. Bronze or green in colour. A summer fish. Needs regular groundbaiting. Baits should be big: bread, worms, sausage, sweetcorn, potato.

Catfish

Imported from Europe. An ugly
fish. Likes slow, warm water and
lots of mud. Grows big and
fights hard when hooked. Will
take worms, deadbait, bread,
cheese, offal, bacon, hard boiled
eggs.

Eel

A summer fish, found
everywhere. Fights hard, even
on the bank, and is very slimy.
Takes worms, meat, offal,
deadbait, bread, strips of fish;
and is not fussy about
freshness. Very tasty when
cooked.

Gudgeon

Looks like a tiny barbel, but has
only two barbules instead of
four, and a speckled body. Likes
clean, running water. Is a strong
fighter on light tackle. Takes
worms, maggots, meat, grubs,
paste.

Roach

The angler's favourite fish. Likes
still or medium-paced water.
Has silver flanks, and a
bluish-green back. Eyes are red
with an orange patch above.
Takes almost any small bait, but
is not greedy, so use groundbait
sparingly.

Tench

Strong, handsome but slimy
fish. Greeny-bronze with
orange-red eyes and a broad
tail. Likes still or slow water, not
too deep, with plenty of mud
and weeds. Takes worms,
maggots, bread, cheese, peas,
wheat, sweetcorn.

Approaching the water

Make your way to the water's edge slowly and
quietly. Fish can see above the surface and feel the
vibration of a heavy footstep: they will move away if
they suspect anything unusual.

How to escape notice
Your clothing should be drab: dark browns and
greens. Use whatever cover there is, including cover
behind you. If you are in front of a bush in drab
clothing, the fish will see the bush, not you. Try to
find a spot in the shade so that your equipment
doesn't catch the light.

Set up your keep net and landing net before you start to fish and make up your rod away from the water. Above all, try to keep low on the horizon all the time you are fishing.

▲The fish's view

Which of the spots illustrated here would you choose to fish from? Check below to see if you are right.

A. BAD: you have no cover and even though you are seated, the fish can still see you.
B. WORSE: you still have no cover and, standing up, are even easier for the fish to spot.
C. BAD: your clothes are too brightly coloured and your shiny rod is catching the light. You will frighten any fish away.

D. GOOD: your drab clothes blend into the background and your rod is matt so it doesn't catch the light.
E. GOOD: you have some cover in front of you but fish may still spot your head and rod against the skyline.
F. BETTER: you have now got complete cover behind you: fish will only see the bush.
G. BEST OF ALL: you are completely hidden by the reeds so your shadow won't fall on the water and scare the fish. From here the fish really can't see you at all.

Care and safety

Angling is a peaceful pastime but there are some dangers. To avoid them always obey these simple rules.

At the waterside
Be careful where you tread; solid-looking ground may shelve inwards and long grass hide a hole. Never wade in deep water, especially not in wellingtons – they can easily fill up and unbalance you.

If you fall in and can't swim, don't panic. Let your natural buoyancy bring you to the surface. Keep your arms under water to help you stay afloat. Don't fight the current, but try to get close enough to the bank to grab a branch; then climb out.

Always weigh fish in a plastic bag. Wet your hands before handling them – dry hands will take off the fish's protective slime.

Your tackle
Hooks can be dangerous, especially on a heavy spinner. Always look behind and around you before casting.

Handling fish
Be very careful handling the fish you catch. If you handle them correctly, they will not feel much pain, and will soon recover when returned to the water. Remember that the fish is suffocating while it is out of the water. If you want to weigh it, do so quickly and gently before slipping it back into the water.

The dorsal fin of a perch or barbel can give you a nasty cut. Pick up the fish with a downward-stroking movement to flatten the fin.

Pike and catfish have razor-sharp teeth. If you are bitten, don't snatch your finger away: that will only engage their backward-pointing teeth.

Chub have powerful throat teeth so only remove a deep-set hook with a disgorger.

Return your catch to the water as gently as possible. Hold it facing the current so that the water flows through its gills. It will soon recover.

Casting

Casting is the method used to send your line and bait out to a chosen spot of water. Very simply, you should take the rod back over your shoulder, bring it forward (as if you were trying to flip a piece of dough off the tip), and release the line so that it follows the bait out over the water. As you can see, there are three basic stages, but you should aim for one continuous movement.

Practise casting on the lawn to get the feel of the rod and the effect of different weights on the line. Don't use hooks. If you are practising with a spinner, tape the hook back for safety. Always look behind you first: for people, trees, bushes and anything else which might be in the way of your line.

**1. Hold the rod with two hands:
the left hand at the bottom of the
butt, the right behind the reel.**

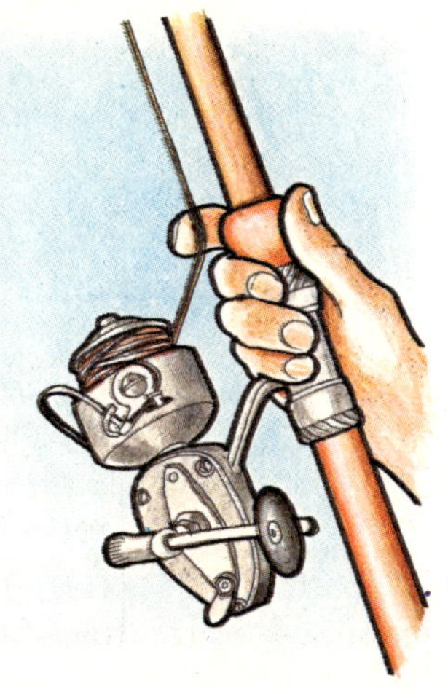

**2. Let the terminal tackle hang
below the rod tip. Clip back the
bale arm. Hold the line with your
right forefinger.**

**3. Now take the rod back over
your right shoulder.**

**4. Bring the line forward,
smoothly but smartly, and take
away your finger. Aim a few feet
above the spot you want to hit.**

**5. Drop the rod tip, checking the
line with your finger if the bait
looks like overshooting. Reset the
bale arm.**

Casting with a centre pin reel

A centre pin reel is the original type of reel which simply winds the line onto a drum. A ratchet holds the line to resist a pulling fish, but can be released to let the reel turn freely for casting and 'trotting' (letting the current carry the bait downstream).

Advantages

You cannot cast as far with a centre pin as you can with a fixed spool reel, but it is much better for trotting, and gives a livelier 'feel' when a fish is being played.

1. Hold the rod across your chest with your right hand. Release the ratchet.

2. With your left hand, strip off a loop of line from the reel. Lift the rod to increase the size.

3. Do this until you are holding several loops of line, then cast out over your chosen spot.

4. Release the loops when the line is fully extended. Unless you are trotting, put the check on.

Float fishing

A float is attached to the line to support the bait at the right depth. When the fish takes the bait, the float bobs down below the surface. The angler then knows that a fish has bitten, and can strike (lifting the rod smartly to hook the fish through the mouth).

Attaching the float
The float is attached to the line by rubber rings at top and bottom. Some floats have wire rings at the bottom, but rubber rings at both ends make changing floats much easier. You can make your own rings (known as float caps) by cutting up rubber bicycle valves.

The float is cocked – kept upright – by split shot. These are balls of lead, split in the middle. They are clipped onto the line below the float.

To make sure the bait is where you want it, you can test the depth of water with a plummet (a bell-shaped lead weight) – see below.

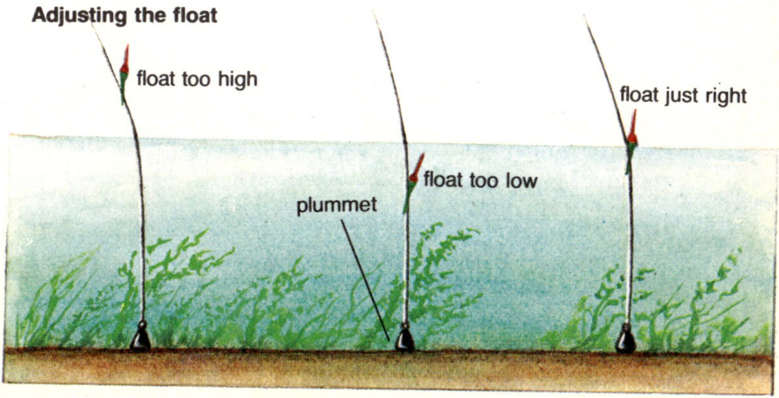

Cast upstream and let the current carry your float past you.

Float fishing on moving water

Always allow for drift when fishing on moving water. Remember that groundbait will drift downstream from the spot where it hits the water. You should normally cast upstream and let the float drift past you some distance downstream. Strike gently in case a fish is biting undetected. Reel in and cast upstream again.

The currents on the surface are faster than those below. The float will be moving ahead of the bait. From time to time tug gently at the float. This will help to get the float drifting *behind* the bait. Otherwise you will have slack line to take up when you strike.

Put your landing net in the water as you bring the fish to the bank.

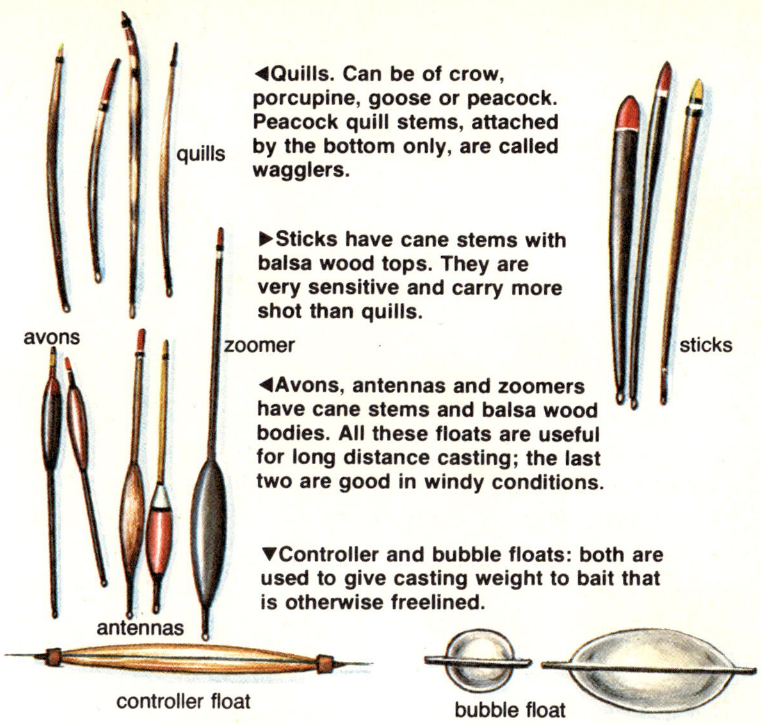

The bite

The float will behave differently according to which fish is biting. A perch 'bobs' it several times before taking it under. Tench or bream will fiddle about for a while. A roach will either pull it down sharply or give it a gentle tug. In general, strike as soon as the float dips underwater. Strike swiftly, but only with enough force to catch the hook in the fish's mouth.

Playing a fish

When playing a fish, keep the rod tip up and the line tight. But be ready to give line to a strong fish. Let the fish do the pulling. Keep the rod tip even as you land the fish. Always bring fish to net; never take net to fish.

Legering

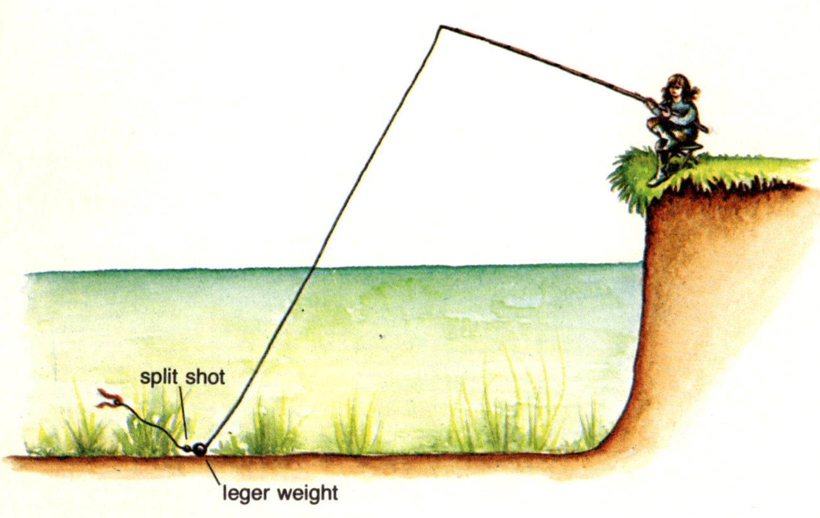

What is legering?

Legering is a way of keeping bait in one place on the bottom, by using a weight and, usually, no float. Thread your line through the hole in the lead weight. Then pinch a split shot onto the line about 45 cm. from the hook to stop the weight from slipping. When you cast, the weight will lie on the bottom.

Leger weights

Choose the lightest weight you need to hold the bait in position. Most popular are the pear lead and the bored bullet. You can make your own leger weight by clipping several large split shot onto a short, looped length of nylon line.

Float leger

Ordinary legering does not involve the use of floats.
But it sometimes helps to add a float to your leger
rig, particularly when fishing beyond weedbeds or
other obstacles where the line might snag.

Find out how deep the water is in the usual way
(see page 33), then attach a float at the correct
distance above the leger weight. The float should be
small and slim, in order to offer as little resistance as
possible to a fish taking the bait.

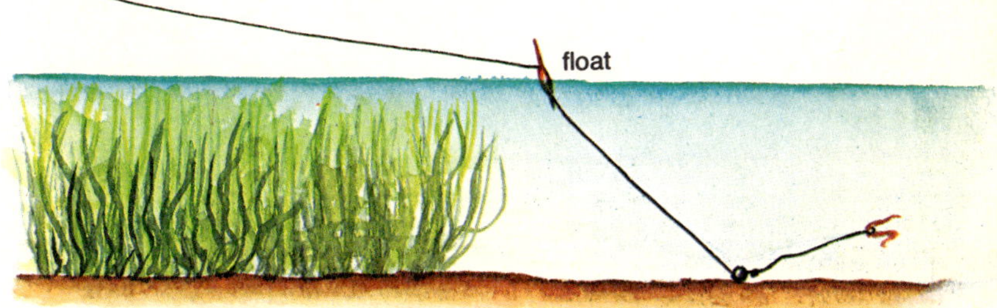

Link leger

This rig involves fixing a leger weight to a length of
nylon line. The other end of the nylon line is
attached to the reel line by a split ring or swivel.

The link leger is especially useful for fishing over
weed or soft mud. The link allows the weight to sink
without pulling the bait down after it.

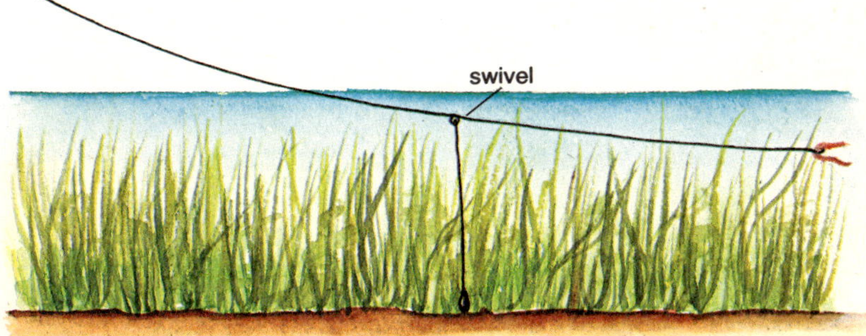

Detecting a bite

Detecting a bite with a leger rig is usually done by touch. If you hold the line between your left thumb and forefinger, you will soon learn to recognize the tell-tale tug.

Artificial aids

However there are also several bite indicators available, which enable you to *see* when a fish is taking the bait. Some of them are illustrated below. You may be able to improvise some others yourself.

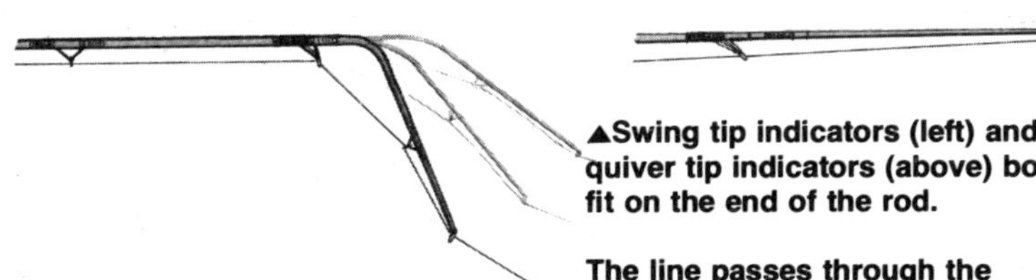

▲Swing tip indicators (left) and quiver tip indicators (above) both fit on the end of the rod.

The line passes through the rings. When a fish bites, the rod tip either swings or quivers.

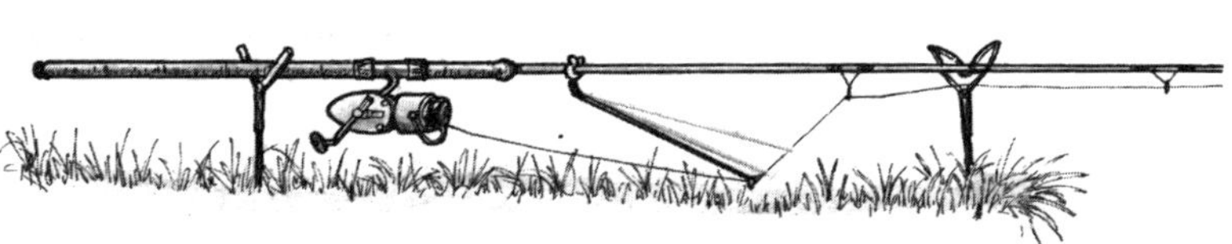

▲A butt bite indicator clips on to the rod. The line passes through the ring at the end. As soon as the fish bites, the indicator lifts up.

▼You can make a dough bobbin by pinching a ball of bread-paste on to the line at either end of the rod. The ball will move when the fish bites.

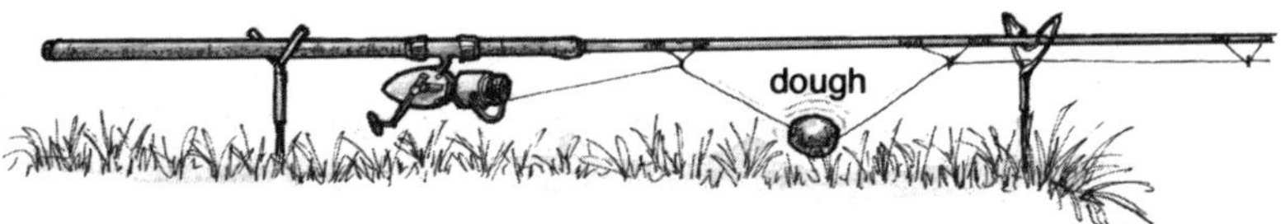

Freelining

Freelining is fishing without a float or weights. It is quite tricky as you have to cast with only the weight of your bait to help you. But it is also very effective: there is no splashing when the bait hits the water, and no bits and pieces on the line to scare away the fish.

Bait for freelining
Freelining can be used on the surface with floating bait: crust, flake, or chrysalis. One excellent method is to hang the bait just over the edge of a lily pad.

Freelining is also very good at middle water level; let a worm sink and then slowly draw it up.

You can also freeline on the bottom with any bait which will sink on its own. Deadbait (small dead fish) are heavy enough to cast a fair distance. They will sink straightaway provided their swim bladders are punctured and the air squeezed out beforehand.

A carp going for a worm.

A rudd attacking a floating crust.

Spinning

Spinning is a very active way of catching predatory fish like pike, perch, zander, chub, trout or salmon. It involves using artificial or dead bait to tempt the fish. The bait is cast out, then reeled back through the water to imitate the movement of a small, weak fish.

The lures

Artificial baits (or 'lures') are made of shiny metal or plastic, with hooks attached to them. They come in many different shapes and sizes. The 'spoon' wobbles as it is drawn through the water. The 'spinner' or 'bar spoon' spins. The 'plug' dives and rises as it is reeled in.

It is worth collecting different types of artificial baits and testing them all. Your prey may find one more tempting than the others.

Artificial baits, like this spinner, look like small, weak fish to the predatory pike.

Deadbait on a single hook. Puncture the swim bladder and add a large shot to the line.

Deadbait on wobble tackle. The body is bent so the bait wobbles when reeled in.

Deadbait

You can also use a real dead fish, called deadbait. This is mounted on a special tackle to make it wobble as it is reeled in. Buy it from your local tackle shop. Types include saltwater fish such as herring and whiting.

You may have even more success with deadbait caught on the water you are fishing. In this way, you will be using a local species which your prey will recognize.

Spinning is a very enjoyable way of fishing. The angler keeps on the move, stalking his prey rather than waiting for it to come to him. Spinning is especially good fun on a cold day when it is uncomfortable to keep still for long periods.

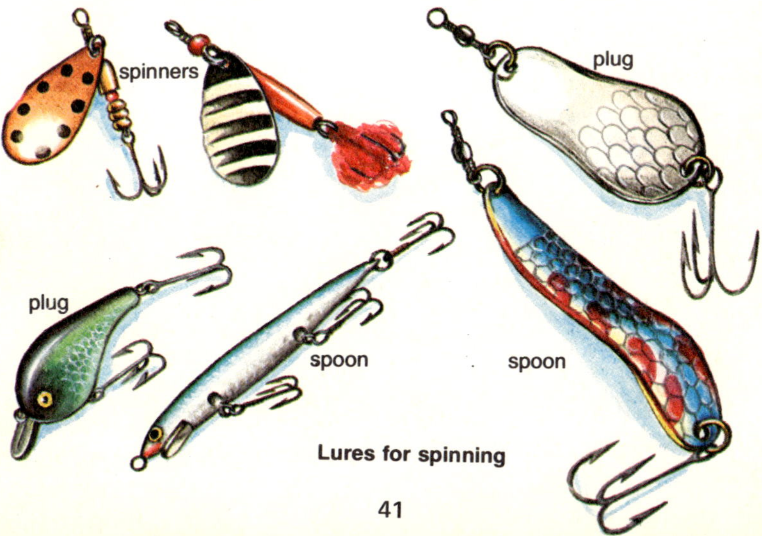

Lures for spinning

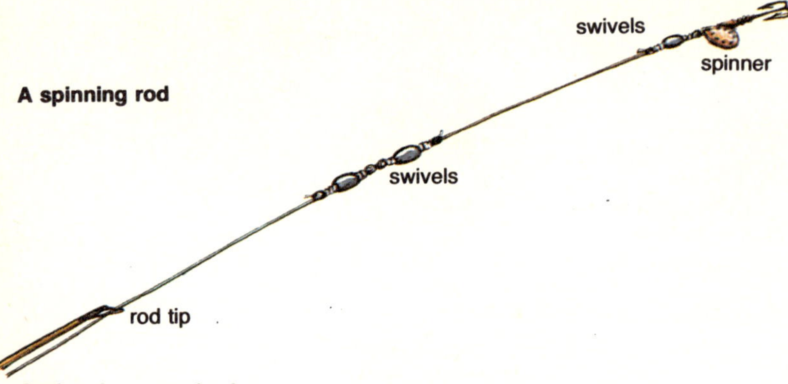

Spinning techniques

Use a spinning rod or a sturdy river rod about 3 metres long. Put swivels on your line to prevent it from kinking as the spinner turns.

When you are fishing for pike, use a length of wire between line and bait, called a 'trace'. It will protect the line from the pike's sharp teeth. Wire traces can be bought ready-made.

Cast out and reel the spinner back towards you. You are meant to be imitating a sickly fish, so vary the speed, letting the line flutter up and down with a 'sink and draw' movement (see below). Don't take it too fast.

To fish a bay or eddy, first cast upstream. Then make each following cast a little further down.

Casting with a spinner

If you can see a fish, cast out some distance away and work the spinner past it. If you can't see one, cast near likely places such as rocks, jetties and bridges, as well as past weedbeds and into eddies.

If there is a current, start by casting well upstream. Then work your way down a long stretch of riverbank, casting repeatedly. Keep an eye open for obstructions: a few lost spinners will add up to an expensive day out.

As soon as you feel a check on the line, strike. You won't mistake a fish's bite: there will be a definite tug on the line.

To cover your own bank, start by casting close by it downstream, then cast a little further out each time.

To fish the far bank of a river cast upstream and work your way down.

Fly fishing

Fly fishing is a very skilled way of catching fish. It can be used for rudd, dace, roach, chub, perch and even pike, as well as salmon, trout and grayling.

The flies

The 'fly' is a hook decorated to look like a real insect or small fish.

There are two kinds of imitation fly: dry and wet. The dry fly floats on the surface. The wet fly goes underwater, imitating a drowned fly or fly larva. A large wet fly or 'fancy' imitates a small fish or shrimp.

Fly fishing is different from other kinds of fishing because there is no weight on the line. The only weight is the line itself which is thick and heavy. A fine nylon 'cast' is tied to the end of the line to take the fly.

FLIES

| Peter Ross (wet) | Drone (dry) | Green Polystickle (wet) | Black Pupa (wet) |
| Dry Cinnamon Sedge (dry) | Green Longhorn (wet) | Brown Lure (wet) | Texas Rose (wet) |

Casting with a fly

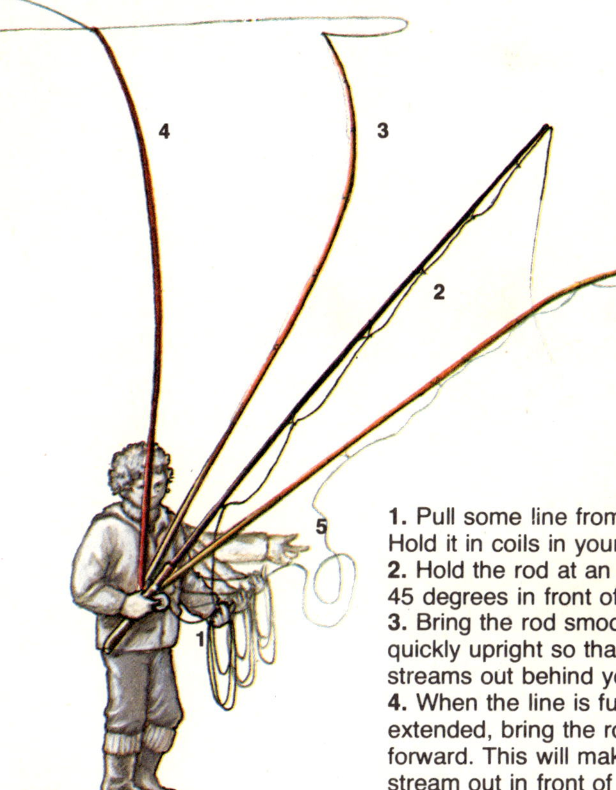

Practise casting on the lawn at home. Don't use a hook: tie a small piece of cloth to the end of the nylon trace.

Start by getting the **feel** of the cast. Then practise for **distance**. Finally, practise for **accuracy**. Put a marker on the lawn and try to hit it. Don't worry if you are way off the mark: fly casting is a tricky business at first.

1. Pull some line from the reel. Hold it in coils in your left hand.
2. Hold the rod at an angle of 45 degrees in front of you.
3. Bring the rod smoothly and quickly upright so that the line streams out behind you.
4. When the line is fully extended, bring the rod smartly forward. This will make the line stream out in front of you.
5. When the line is straight out in front, release the coils in your left hand.
6. Drop the rod tip when the fly is about a metre above the target.

Casting further out
To cast further out from the bank, keep repeating all but the last movement, pulling more line from the reel each time, until you have reached your target.

Fishing for trout

Before you go fishing on any trout water, make sure you have the necessary permission. Trout are delicious to eat, but there is a size limit on most waters: undersized trout must be returned to the water. Trout will take many kinds of bait, especially worms. But on many waters you are only allowed to use flies. Check *before* you start fishing.

Fishing with a dry fly
The dry fly is used on smooth water. Oil both line and fly with a floatant to keep them on the surface. Cast upstream and take in slack line as the fly floats towards you. Then pay out the line as it floats past you downstream.

If you see a ring of water made by a rising fish, cast upstream of it and let the fly float over it. Do not strike as soon as the fish's head breaks water. Wait a split second until it has taken the fly.

Fishing with a wet fly

The wet fly is used on rough water. The fly is
wetted before casting to make it sink. In fast water
you may need to add some copper wire to the line to
make it sink.

With a wet fly, cast downstream and across to the
opposite bank. Check the line to make the current
swing the fly back to your own bank. If there have
been no bites by the time it reaches the bank, take
in the line in short, sharp tugs.

When wet fly fishing on a lake, cast around beds
of reed or weed, and under overhanging trees. Work
the fly by sinking and drawing it repeatedly.

Fishing from a boat

Fishing from a boat greatly increases your range, and enables you to reach all kinds of out of the way spots.

You will still be fishing mainly towards the bank: that's where most of the fish will be. But you can also fish around patches of weed in midstream, or under trees or overhanging banks and tangled undergrowth.

Equipment
Take only essential gear and arrange it evenly around the boat. Make up your rod before setting out, and don't use one much more than three metres long. Use a short-handled landing net.

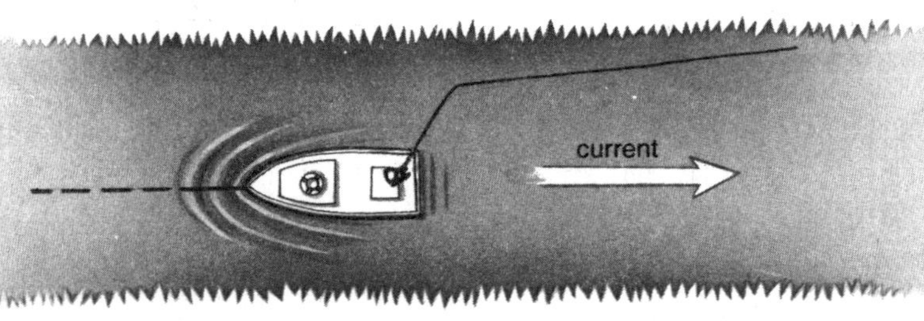

▲Fish downstream. If you are on your own, fish from the stern of the boat.

▼If there are two of you in a boat, space yourselves out evenly.

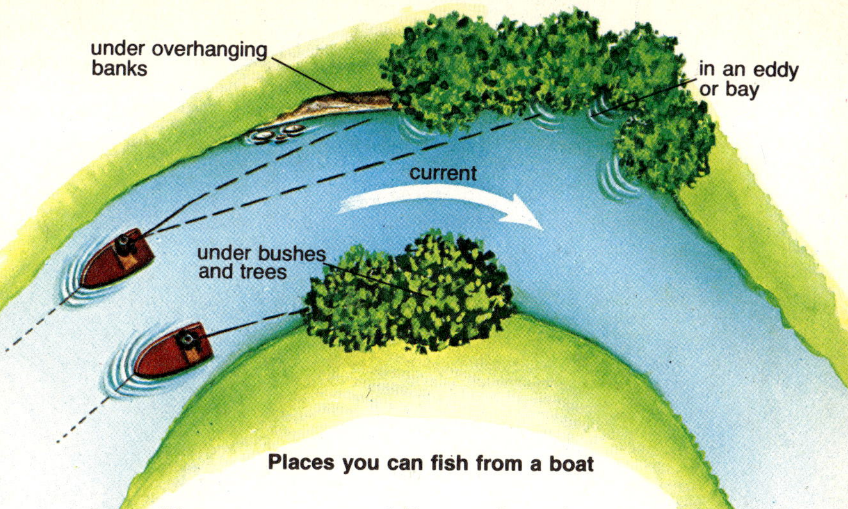

Places you can fish from a boat

On still water, use paddles rather than oars: they splash less. Stop paddling well above your chosen fishing spot and drift down towards it. Anchor quietly in the shade where there is no strong current.

Precautions

Always fish downstream, otherwise the current will bring your tackle back towards (or under) your boat. Never knock anything against the side of your boat: the vibrations will scare the fish. Move about as little as possible. Always hold on to the side of the boat.

Safety in boats

Always wear a life jacket. Wear rope or rubber-soled shoes, not wellingtons. If there are several people in the boat, space yourselves evenly. To change places, move one at a time. Never, never, stand up.

On waterways, keep to the right and close to the bank.

Never cut across the bows of an approaching craft.

If you do fall in and are far from the bank, **stay with the boat.**

If it gets very windy, point the boat into the wind and head for the bank. Forget trying to reach the point you started from: just get back to the bank.

Knots for anglers

The right knot can make all the difference between landing a fish and losing it. Practise knotting until you can do it with your eyes shut. When fishing you may have to tie knots in bad light, in rain, and with hands that are stiff and cold. Nylon lines are almost invisible. They are a lot trickier to tie than ordinary string.

These drawings show the knots tied loosely. Remember that you must pull them very, very tight.

The blood bight
The blood bight is used to make a simple loop on the end of a cast or reel line (see right).

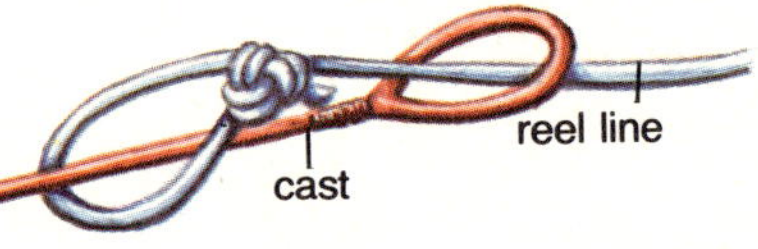

1. Bend the end of the line double.

The **four-turn blood knot** is used to join two lengths of line.

2. Twist the loop back around the line.

3. Pull the loop back again.

The **four-turn half blood knot** is a secure way of attaching eyed hooks or swivels to a line.

The **turle knot** is useful for attaching eyed hooks to the line.

Whipping knot
This is good for replacing broken rod rings.

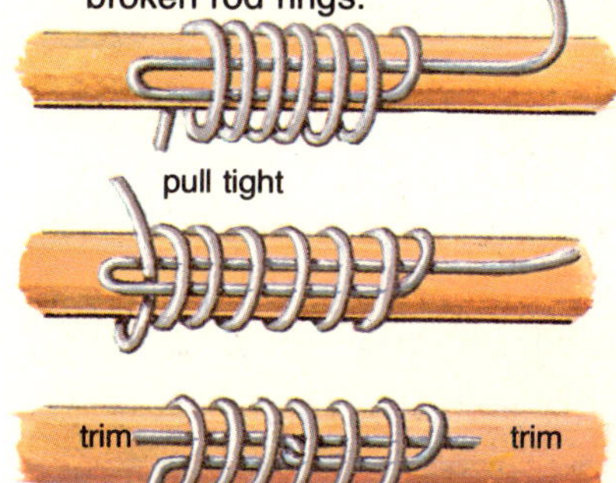

The domhof knot   This gives a strong grip on the shank of an eyed hook.

To make a whipping knot
Wind the thread around the rod and the 'leg' of the ring, as in the diagrams above. Push the end through the loop and pull tight. Then trim the ends.

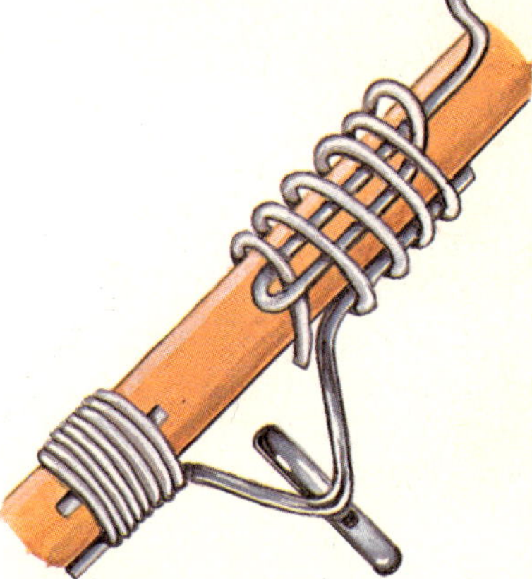

Spade-end knot   Spade-end hooks have flattened sections instead of eyes. Try this spade-end knot to secure them to the line.

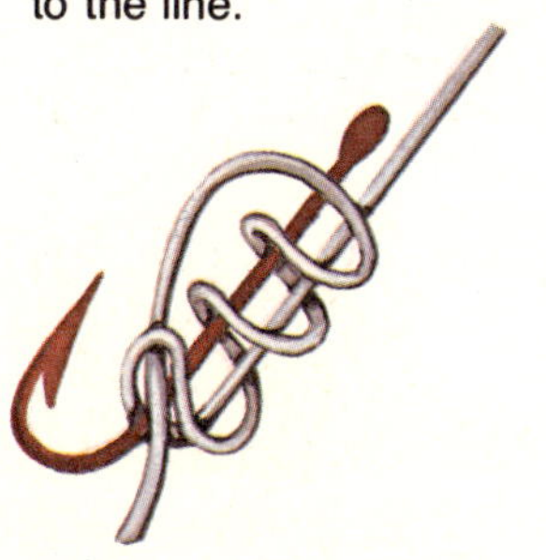

The illustrations above only show the principle of the whipping knot. You will need to wind the thread round many more times. The threads should be pulled very tight.

Making your own tackle

Making a quill float

1. Find a feather and strip the fibres from the quill.

2. Paint the top. Stick the quill in a crust of bread till dry. Turn it over and paint the rest. Then varnish it.

3. Attach rubber float caps, or whip on a shop-bought float eye to the bottom. (For whipping knot see page 51.)

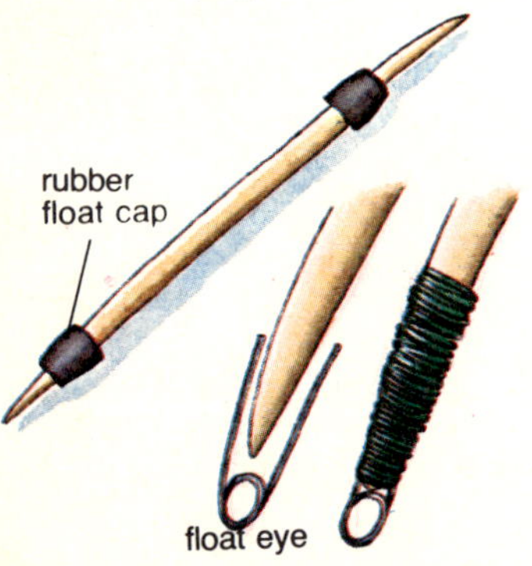

Making an Avon float

1. Buy lengths of cane and drilled balsa from a tackle shop.

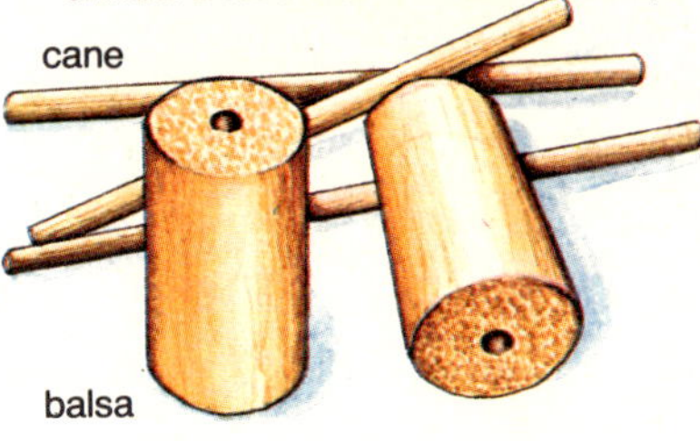

2. Coat cane with epoxy resin glue and stick through the balsa.

3. Round off the ends with a craft knife.

4. Finish shaping with an emery board. Paint the float with enamel paint and varnish when dry.

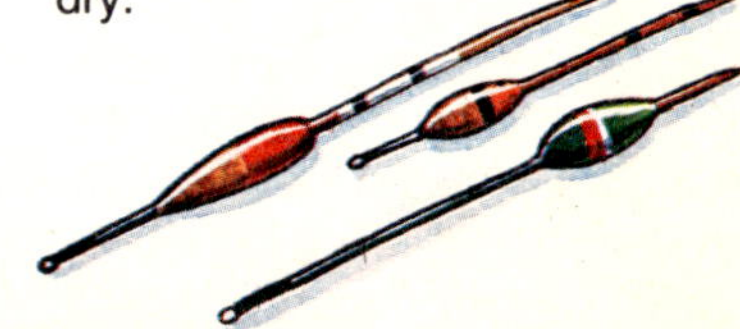

Making a self-cocking float

1. Cut a length of peacock quill. Cut the bottom off a goose quill.
2. Put two or three shot in the bottom of the goose quill. Push it on to the peacock quill.
3. Test in a jam jar for the amount of shot needed to cock the float. Adjust if necessary. Dismantle and dry. Glue, paint and varnish.

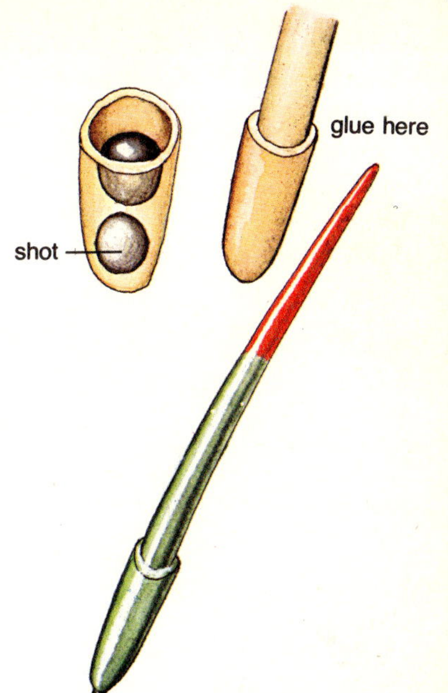

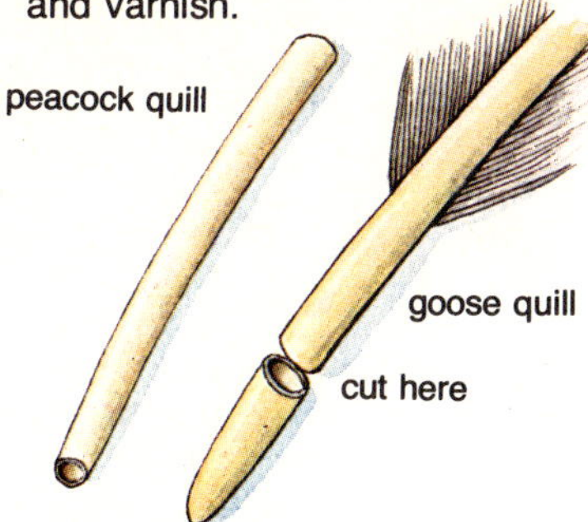

Making a rod rest

1. Take a piece of coathanger wire about 45 cm. long. Bend into shape, as shown. Twist the ends together and bind them with insulating tape (**2**).
3. Coat the tape with epoxy resin glue and push into the hollow top of a bamboo cane (**4**).

OR: keep the ends straight and tape them to the top of a sharp stick. Sharpen the other end into a point.

Making a slow-sink leger weight

Trim a small cork into an egg shape. Cut a groove around the middle. Wrap lead wire around the groove. Cut a hole in the bottom of the cork to take a large split shot.

Clip a shot onto a length of nylon. Thread nylon through the cork, pulling shot into hole. Seal hole with glue mixed with cork dust. Add a swivel to the free end of nylon.

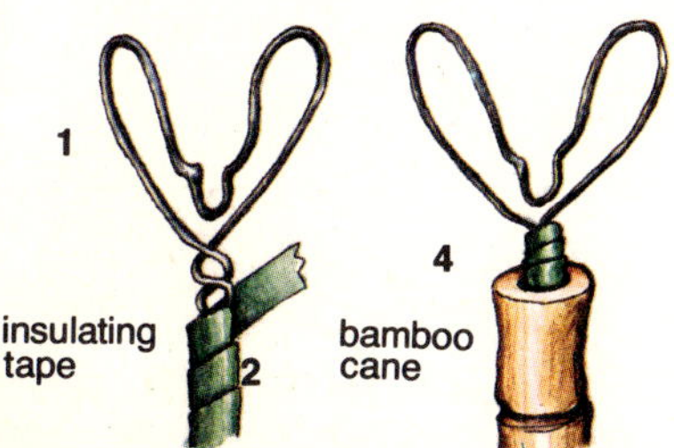

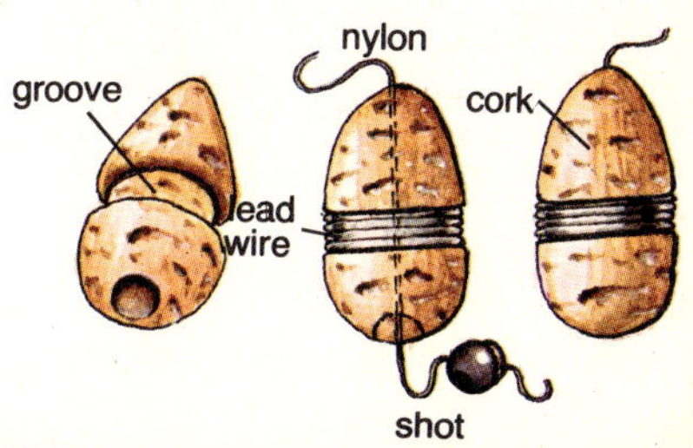

Animals of the waterside

As you sit quietly fishing by the waterside, you will gradually become part of the landscape. Wild animals and birds, normally frightened, will go about their lives around you. But please don't expect to see all the creatures in this picture at once!

If you are lucky you may find a robin perched on your rod tip, or a water vole sampling your discarded bait. Or perhaps an otter may climb on to a boulder with a fish gripped tight between his teeth. Learn to recognize the animals you see, and turn your fishing trip into a nature trail.

swallow
swift
dragonfly
kingfisher
heron
swan
mallard
coot
moorhen
water rat

A fishing notebook

Keeping records

A fishing notebook helps you to plan ahead. If you record the number and kinds of fish you have caught at different times and places, you will notice a pattern emerging.

You may find, for example, that a certain stretch of water was good for bream at one time but hopeless at another.

Note down places, times, catches, baits and weather conditions.

Other ideas

You can draw sketch **maps** of different stretches of water and stick in any **photographs** you have taken. And why not include the **spinner** with which you caught some monster pike! Stick in **pressed leaves and flowers** too, with notes on other vegetation.

There is plenty to include. And when the fishing season ends, you will have a colourful record of an enjoyable season.

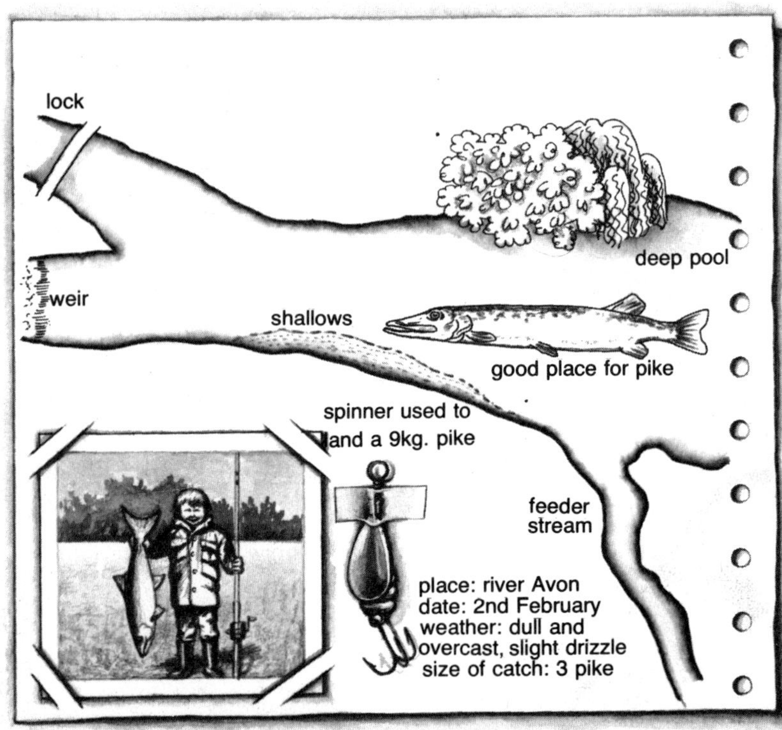

Making a map

Using maps
Maps will help you to build up a picture of the way fish behave on a particular stretch of water (or swim). As the information builds up you will discover that particular 'swims' mean guaranteed success, or failure.

Information to include
Include as much information as you can. Note down exactly where you caught each different species of fish.

Samples
Take samples of weed by running a spinner through it. Find out what insects live in it. A plummet smeared with petroleum jelly will bring up bits from the bottom for you to identify the type of soil.

Depth soundings
You can map out the depth of the bottom by taking soundings with a plumb line, or a plummet on float tackle.

A code
To avoid crowding your map, work out a code with symbols for the different features.

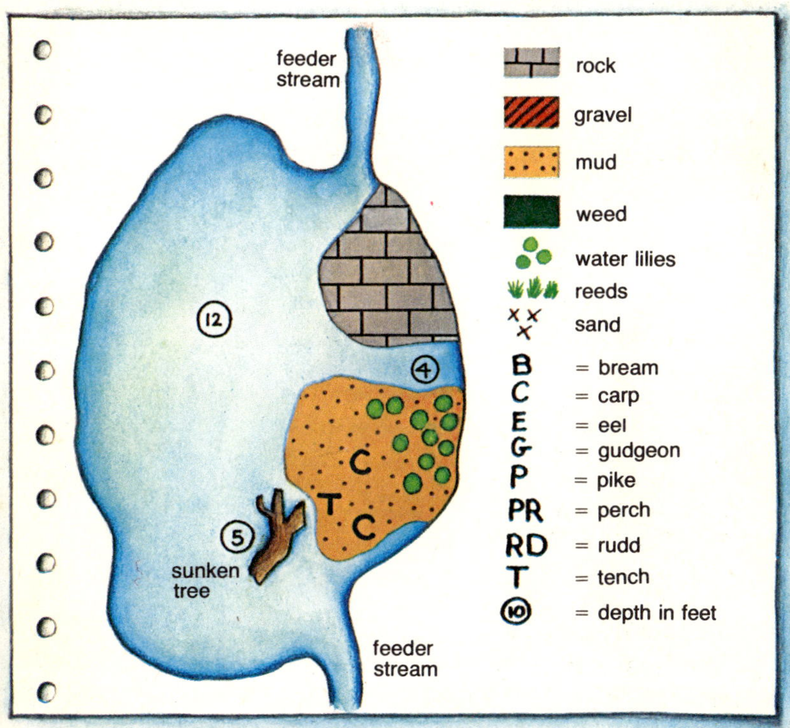

Reference section

Joining a club

You can greatly increase your enjoyment of fishing by joining an angling club.

Most clubs have a special Junior Section at reduced membership fees for anglers under 16 and are very keen to encourage younger members.

You should be able to get a list of the clubs in your area from your local library. If not, write to:

The National Anglers' Council,
5 Cowgate,
Peterborough PE1 1LR.

What can the club do for you?
The best thing is that the club will have its own water or waters which you can fish without extra charge. The club may be affiliated, or linked, with one of the very big clubs such as the London Anglers' Association, which will allow you to fish their waters as well.

It will arrange matches against junior sections of other clubs and organize trips to distant waters. You will meet lots of other young anglers and be able to swap ideas and information.

Bait and tackle may be bought in bulk by the club, and offered to members at special low prices.

Most clubs have coaching sessions and talks given by experienced anglers, so you will be able to improve your knowledge and skills very quickly indeed. In any case, the older anglers are always ready to offer advice.

What does club membership mean?
You can join in club activities like clearing, weeding and dredging waters; collecting litter from the banks; pegging out match stretches; selling raffle tickets, and painting the clubhouse – in fact anything which needs willing helpers.

Some projects, such as netting fish for transfer to other waters, will be interesting, others may be less so. But even boring jobs have to be done – and you will always have the satisfaction of repaying the club a little for the enjoyment it is giving you.

Useful addresses

To fish any water you will need an annual rod licence as well as your club membership or day ticket. Contact the Recreation and Amenity Officer at your regional Water Authority for licences and any other information.

The organizations listed below have an interest in angling and will be glad to offer help, advice and information.

The different **tourist boards** will supply information on fishing holidays and the best areas in which to fish. The **National Anglers' Council** will help with names of clubs in different areas. It is also the judge of whether or not you have caught a record fish (*see page 60*). Finally, membership of the **Youth Hostels Association** will prove useful if you plan to fish in out of the way places.

Anglers' Co-operative
  Association,
Midland Bank Chambers,
Westgate,
Grantham,
Lincs.

Central Council of Physical
  Recreation,
70 Brompton Road,
London SW3 1HE.

English Tourist Board,
4 Grosvenor Gardens,
London SW1 0DU.

Inland Waterways Association,
114 Regent's Park Road,
London NW1 8UQ.

Irish Tourist Board,
15 New Bond Street,
London W1Y 0AG.

National Anglers' Council
  (and Record (Rod-caught)
  Fish Committee)
5 Cowgate,
Peterborough PE1 1LR.

Northern Ireland Tourist
  Board,
11 Berkeley Street,
London W1X 6BU.

Scottish Tourist Board,
23 Ravelston Terrace,
Edinburgh EH4 3EU.

Sports Council,
70 Brompton Road,
London SW3 1EX.

Welsh Tourist Centre,
Glamorgan Street,
Brecon.

Youth Hostels Association,
Trevelyan House,
St Stephen's Hill,
St Albans,
Herts.

British records for freshwater fish

The British Record Fish Committee of the National Anglers' Council (*see page 59*) decides on the claims for record fish (both fresh and salt water) caught with a rod in United Kingdom waters. At least once a year it publishes a list of the records.

Claims for records have to be made in writing to the Secretary of the Committee, stating:
(i) the species of fish and the weight;
(ii) the date and place of capture, and the tackle used;
(iii) the names and addresses of reliable witnesses, both to the capture of the fish and the weight.

If you catch what you think may be a record fish and there are no witnesses on the bank, take the fish (alive if possible) to your nearest tackle dealer, who will be glad to weigh and witness the catch. The fish must then be kept for examination.

Some fish records
Bream
Weight: 13lb 8oz (6.123kg)
Date: 1977

Chub
Weight: 7lb 6oz (3.345kg)
Date: 1957

Eel
Weight: 11lb 2oz (5.926kg)
Date: 1978

Gudgeon
Weight: 4oz 4dm (120g)
Date: 1977

Perch
Weight: 4lb 12oz (2.154kg)
Date: 1962

Pike
Weight: 40lb (18.143kg)
Date: 1967

Roach
Weight: 4lb 1oz (1.824kg)
Date: 1975

Rudd
Weight: 4lb 8oz (2.041kg)
Date: 1933

Salmon
Weight: 64lb (29.029kg)
Date: 1922

Tench
Weight: 10lb 1oz (4.564kg)
Date: 1975

Brown Trout
Weight: 19lb 9oz (8.873kg)
Date: 1978

Rainbow Trout
Weight: 19lb 8oz (8.844kg)
Date: 1977

Glossary

Bait: anything used to attract fish.

Hookbait: used on the hook.

Groundbait: a mixture thrown into the water to land on the bottom.

Cloudbait: a fine mixture which forms a cloud in the water.

Deadbait: whole or part of a dead fish.

Bite detector: device used on the line which signals a bite.

Breaking strain: the weight a fishing line can take without breaking.

Cast: swinging the rod and line to put a baited hook into the water; a length of finer line between the hook and the reel line.

Caster: the newly formed chrysalis of a maggot. (An older chrysalis is called a **floater**.)

Disgorger: device for removing a hook from a fish's mouth.

Flies: hooks dressed with feathers to imitate insects.

Float: buoyant object used to support the bait and warn the angler of a bite.

Freelining: fishing without float or weights.

Lateral line: row of nerve endings on a fish's flank through which it picks up vibrations.

Leads: weights used on the line in float and leger fishing.

Legering: method of fishing where the line runs through a hole in a weight.

Rolling leger: a form of legering in which the weight is allowed to roll about on the bottom.

Link leger: uses a length of line to attach the leger weight to the reel line.

Roach pole: a long rod without a reel.

Sink and draw: a deliberate up and down movement of the bait.

Spinning: fishing with the help of a moving artificial bait.

Strike: the upward movement of the rod which sets the hook in the fish's mouth.

Swim: the stretch of water an angler fishes in.

Booklist

The following list is a guide to other books about fishing. They will help to increase your interest and improve your angling skills. Your local library should be able to order most of them for you:

The Anglers' Encyclopaedia by Colin Willock (Pelham Books, 1978)

A.A. Guide to Angling in Great Britain (A.A./Octopus Books, 1977)

Coarse Fishing by N. Scott (Ladybird Books, 1969)

Coarse Fishing for New Anglers by W. M. Hill (David & Charles, 1975)

Coarse Fishing for Beginners by Kenneth Mansfield (Foulsham, 1974)

Coarse Fishing Round Britain (Aquarius Books, 1977)

Fishing for Beginners by Maurice Wiggin (Dent, 1962)

Fishing with David Carl Forbes (Hamlyn, 1976)

Fishing with the Experts by Hugh Stoker, Fred J. Taylor, John Neville (David & Charles, 1978)

Fly Fishing by Maurice Wiggin (Hodder & Stoughton, 1977)

How to Start Coarse Fishing by Peter Tombleson (Ernest Benn, 1976)

Illustrated Teach Yourself Coarse Fishing by Peter Stone (Knight Books, 1977)

The Pursuit of Stillwater Trout by Brian Clarke (Pan Books, 1978)

Stillwater Angling by Richard Walker (Pan Books, 1975)

Stillwater Fly Fishing by T. C. Ivens (Pan Books, 1973)

Teach Yourself Coarse Angling by Cliff Parker (Hodder & Stoughton, 1976)

Where to Fish 1978–79 by D. A. Orton (Harmsworth Press, 1978)

Index